I have been called a Traitor by my Nemesis

A Philosophical Poetry Book

Hugo Jepsen

Preface

'Freedom can savour the mind but arrogance can lead you to death' — this was the first thought that came into my mind when I started sketching '*I have been called a Traitor by my Nemesis*'.

This book compiles several philosophical theories written in poetry such as hedonism, karmic relationships, epiphanies, and deja vu; it also touches on issues such as depression, climate change, sustainability, and hardships in school, anxiety within relationships, and many more.

I found myself deeply inspired to create a poetic view of all these subjects as an attempt of self-expression in hopes that the readers can relate to and understand things they, perhaps, previously didn't understand.

Chapters:

Bonus Chapters (Paperback Exclusive)

fly but not too high

Freedom can savour the mind
but arrogance can lead to death
and even I exercise caution when I fly,
so be careful to not take the wrong steps.

But, you must not soar too high,
for the atmosphere will burn your wings.
I know, I know, the sky looks to be so close,
but you know, you know, it's out of your reach.

Wary of causing damage altogether,
that's a completely different matter,
yet, caution is what brought you here,
not the strength of your own feathers.

But you say, 'I flew here, I'm flying now,
and look at how all problems have become'.
But, foolish you, have forgotten something —
you and the world can never be as one.

you only see the horizon

The eternal summer ocean
and the wide blue sky above -
if all these things don't feel exciting,
sorry to say, you can't understand love.

As for love, a true paradise in the sea,
where the ships navigate through,
but if yet, you can't understand me,
then, I might not understand you.

The horizon races up your heart,
desiring for a safe shore at its end,
but as long as you keep diving,
there will be things you haven't seen yet.

It is really an amazing sight at the front —
the happiness of meeting the prize
is that you've forgotten the reasoning,
you just cared about finishing it ahead of time.

class of traitors

Falling into a class of traitors
when one is the worst traitor of all
is nothing but a rat race in prison
within a competition at its default.

Every man or every woman who
has lied to themselves to ease the pain
has done nothing but betray themselves through
foolish attempts to live life the better way.

Because when the rain falls above our heads,
we open umbrellas to protect ourselves instead -
instead of letting the natural flow, flow naturally within us,
and that's the paradox of life and all of its because.

my anxiety is destroying our relationship

I carved in a tree, your name,
so my heart can find a stable ground
when your passion makes me feel insane.

You've given up the heaven above,
so you could save me from the hell I live in -
if that is not love, what then? what is it?

I just want to live in this moment forever,
but I'm afraid if I don't get any better,
I'll be missing out on us being together.

And I apologize for all the mistakes,
my anxiety is destroying our relationship -
and I am so sorry.

we are travellers walking across the Earth

To have power and fail to use it
is the same as the behaviour of a fool -
as for choices that are made recklessly
is the consequence of being called cruel.

We are travellers walking across
the room we like to call Earth,
yet, we've destroyed its furniture
for the sake of comfort and not of love.

We break and destroy the things we cherish
with only one premise in mind - to make them better.
However - is making them better necessary
to be comfortable to avoid any future pressure?

The fish in the river swim with the currents
following the natural course of their birthplace,
but we, the humankind, evolved in a way
which we feel entitled to all of this world's space.

apricot taste

Apricot is the way that you taste,
thinking sweet when it's your or was your mistake
and all your words have become tongue-tied
because when you speak the truth, you've lied.

The fire you started when you burnt my book
has caused your heart to burst into flames
because no matter where you look,
you seem to only recognize my name.

But you've forgotten your place in the world,
your treasure hunting was found by me.
And at the end of it all, you've got nothing,
but I, on the other hand, was set free.

Because the apricot started to taste better
when I picked it up, all by myself,
and that book that you burnt
has returned to my shelf.

the village is made out of the dirt

You've built a village from the green side
that you've forgotten that dirt is brown.
Perhaps, you were running out of time
to notice that, that village was my hometown.

And 'from the dirt, you shall return' - something so -
but I haven't returned that favour to you, also.
Because, if you attempt to dig deep beneath the ground,
minerals, gems and other crystals may be found.

You're delirious now, or even, excited perhaps,
the eyes of someone looking bright at things that shine
was the mistake you made when you attempted to
leave what doesn't serve you - but you've only tried.

If you've only tried but you've never accomplished anything,
there's no middle ground between your legs and your feet
because the only good thing you've achieved so far
was creating a faultline between you and me.

relationship amnesia

Have we ever been in a relationship?
I'm not sure, I do not think so.
Have I ever been crushed down?
That's it, that's so but that also.

However, if I leave my worries in your care,
I might end up sulking feelings out of nowhere -
and if I get tongue-tied suddenly
it's because I know of you, personally.

abyss

I went to the abyss the other day
to try to find something rare -
what I only found was
my own spectrum of despair.

Negligence is the word I miss out
every time someone gets close to me,
but if despair wasn't what I had found,
perhaps, I'd have someone on my knees.

Careless was the apathy that consumed
all the potential gains I could've won,
but instead, I made the mistake
of trying to solve realism alone.

I came back to the abyss once again,
I think I'll stay here for quite a while,
hoping that someone would have the courage
to meet me, even when it feels hostile.

you've been changing but it's not enough

You said you can do it all night,
said that I was walking out of line,
but I can't make any excuses for you,
and for you, I can't put my trauma to the side.

Had me feeling like I've died,
I've never seen a man cry
like when I saw myself doing so,
and the fault is yours - you know?

And I see you've been changing,
trying to be more of my taste.
And I see you've been chasing,
but I think now it's far too late.

And you know, you messed me up,
we'll never be friends like this,
hating me won't make me love,
wanting me it's nothing special,
exes like you and me don't become sexual.

a meteor killed her daughter

The old widow goes to the land
where she was once forgotten
as for her, it's incandescently painful
to remember that a meteor killed her daughter.

I am leaving her memories behind —
what was destroyed in the past
can't ever come back to life.

Yet, she prays, she's hopeful
but in her case, I could never be,
because I can't be someone
who feels different from me.

hedonism

If I wanted to know who you've been with,
I would have asked you if you have been -
long ago, if it ever mattered, jealous I'd get,
but perhaps, it's my hedonism or lack of care.

The end.

my sadness has become beautiful

When tears are running down,
I have found no ways to stop it -
it's from tears that I'm all about.

I held your hand, too strong, I think,
I find the pain to become quite beautiful,
but I don't think you share the same feeling.

And when my tears run over you,
you make it all about bad luck
instead of taking responsibility for the things you do.

Yet, I held your hand way too strong,
I think I didn't tell you that I was scared,
but I just wanted to keep me inside your chest.

green branches

The green branches of olive trees
are growing themselves to
pierce their roots inside of me —
what am I supposed to do?

The semblance of the shade
and the yearning they utterly make
and the gripping sound
that I hear whenever they break.

And they've broken out
inside a body that is mine —
all the words they tell me about
are about tipping points in time.

They've pierced through
and we've become one —
the way that I feel the world
is the way that we've become —
and baby, it burns, I feel it burn.

hug the roots of a tree

Hug the roots
of a single tree
if you ever need me.

Put your head up to the sky
to just let the rain
touch your face
when you want to wash your pain away.

And let the sun burn
the depths of your heart
to let yourself free
for you and me, to restart.

killing me tonight

It hurts me so much within,
I just feel my heart getting thin,
And I feel a stroke inside of me,
I want to get out of me, away with it.

I feel some rainbows for real,
But I never accepted such a deal.
I feel some gold in your touch,
But it was never ever enough.

I feel some passion inside my bones,
But it was never really shown,
And I feel your warmth at night,
Even if you're sleeping outside.

And all the memories kept above
Are coming back so strong this time
That all I feel now is just love
And that love is killing me tonight.

invisible scars

I see monsters in the clouds,
piano sounds sounding so loud,
sometimes, I can't get it out,
but sometimes I live in the now.

dark forests hollowing me behind,
all the steps I've taken in this life,
cowboys and horse tamers allied,
probably, coming for what's mine.

I had shields around me of iron,
somehow you broke it entirely,
with lies covered in red and blue,
I'm the origin of what you can do.

And you can paint art, drive cars,
beat up me with hammers
while leaving invisible scars,
and to last, send me to the stars.

speechless words

I've covered myself
between the sheets -
the outdoors look better
if they never see me.

I see the light coming undone,
I've done nothing, yet always around -
when the raindrops take over my place,
it uncovers the secrets of my hometown.

I see the kindness in your evil,
I feel the depths of your soul
but you decided to stay
and I left the best person I've ever known.

Speechless words are also words -
I sit by the window, sitting in hurt,
tears seem to spill over my clothes -
I guess passion isn't the same as love.

hoax

If you can't sleep at night,
it's because I'm screaming
your name to the sky.

If you can't be awake,
it's because I'm here
dreaming about your face.

If I can't hold my tears,
hold me tight,
and understand my fears.

But if I die for you,
don't cry about it.
It will be about love
and I'll be looking to,
to you from above.

Credits

Writer: Hugo Jepsen
Editor: Hugo Jepsen
Cover Creator: Hugo Jepsen
Image License: Unsplash
Publisher: Amazon

Disclaimer

Any resemblance to other creative projects is mere coincidence.

Copyrights

Protected and Licensed with a Copyright Infringement.